BENEFITS OF PRAYING IN TONGUES

KINGDOM DYNAMICS FOR BREAKTROUGH

STEPHEN A. GARNER

Benefits of Praying In Tongues

Stephen A. Garner

Rivers Publishing Company
Chicago, IL

TABLE OF CONTENTS

FOREWORD

I count it a great honor to write these words for this exciting book written by my spiritual father in Christ, Apostle Stephen A. Garner. I am personally indebted to him for the spiritual strength and insights I have received from God through this great Apostle. He has a unique ability to search out the scriptures and bring out revelatory truth that, if embraced, will change your life eternally. I can only pray and hope that many believers [and unbelievers too!] will find this book coming into their hands and drawing from it; the amazing spiritual truths that these pages contain.

Apostle Rod L. Stevenson
Rivers of Living Water Ministries International
Grand Rapids, MI USA

INTRODUCTION

Praying in Tongues has remained a hot topic of debate and a subject that has been shroud with mysticism for many generations within the Church. I endeavor to bring revelatory insight that will enlighten those who desire to advance in the things of God. Today, many denominations have instructed us to only speak in tongues, if an interpreter is present. We have also heard that we should only speak, as the Spirit of God gives us utterance. These assertions may hold true in both cases. Yet, as we look at tongues as being a prayer language, these claims become unwarranted.

The Word of God is clear on this subject. On the day of Pentecost, in Acts 2, there came a tangible manifestation of spiritual power upon the believers. God broke into the earth realm and began to knit His people together as never before by the release of *Other Tongues*. Those **unlearned** in foreign languages were able to articulate the language of their brethren by the Spirit of God. Here, we can see from the scriptures that *Unknown Tongues* are also a critical part of our ministry to the Lord; because **it is a language which no man can interpret**. Only the Father knows the interpretation of this glorious language according to I Corinthians 14:2. *"For he that speaketh in an unknown tongue speaketh not unto men, but unto God: for no man understandeth him; howbeit in the spirit he speaketh mysteries"*.

I believe the level of discouragement is at an all time high in the Body of Christ because the devil has been successful in keeping the Church divided on foundational truths. The fact is the Church has been fighting itself so fiercely, only to remain carnal, relays a message to God that we choose to refuse to be spiritual. This issue has reached the point where we deny ourselves of our right to pray to God the Father in the heavenly language He has given to us. The Lord Jesus has paid the ultimate price in His blood and provided us with benefits in the here and now. I pray that you will gain these invaluable tools and receive the benefits that God has made available to every believer.

Apostle Stephen A. Garner
Rivers of Living Water Ministries International
Chicago, IL USA

BENEFIT #1

PRAYING IN TONGUES BRINGS TIMES OF REST AND REFRESHING

"For with stammering lips and another tongue will he speak to this people. To whom he said, This is the rest wherewith ye may cause the weary to rest; and this is the refreshing: yet they would not hear."   **Isaiah 28:11-12**

The historical passage of Isaiah 28:11-12 addresses the Assyrians who had become rulers and teachers in the nation of Israel. Due to Israel's leadership's negligence in obeying the commandments of the Lord, they found themselves in bondage to the Assyrians. What replaced the rest of the Lord became the rod of an oppressive nation upon God's people. Prophetically, I believe that as we pray in tongues, demonic oppression will be broken off our lives, families, ministries, cities, regions, and ultimately our nations. The key to accessing the rest and refreshing of the Lord is linked to our ability to exercise our spiritual language by faith. In *The Moffat Translation*, verse 11 reads, *"Yes and through stammering lips and in a foreign tongue will God talk to this people." The American Translation* states, *"Yes through barbaric lips and an alien tongue will He speak through this people."* We can now determine that our prayer language is a means for God to communicate His will and release His counsel into the earth. Let us examine the following scripture in other biblical translations.

Isaiah 28:12.

"The God who told them once, where true rest lay, rest for worn souls, refreshing rest, and they would not listen." **The Moffat Translation**

"To whom he said, this is the rest, give ye rest to him that is weary, and this is the refreshing yet they would not hear" **The American Translation**

"He once told them: here is rest: let the weary rest. Here is repose. But they would not listen." **The Jerusalem Translation**

"This people to whom he once said this is true rest, let the exhausted have true rest. This is repose and they refuse to listen." **The New English Bible**

From these various translations, we understand our need to be refreshed because of the weariness that sometimes comes from doing well. The bible also warns us of the fact that the devil will *seek to wear out the Saints of the Most High.* Physical and spiritual exhaustion comes as you carry your cross during times of indifference, tribulation, warfare and the trial of our faith; to name a few. The act of praying in tongues benefits us and brings the rest and refreshing that is so needed in the lives of believers to help us rise above, outmaneuver, overcome, and eventually withstand the forces of darkness.

BENEFIT #2

PRAYING IN TONGUES BIRTHS PROPHETIC FULFILLMENT

"And when the day of Pentecost had fully come, they were all assembled together in one place, 2 When suddenly there came a sound from heaven like the rushing of a violent tempest blast, and it filled the whole house in which they were sitting. 3 And there appeared to them tongues resembling fire, which were separated and distributed and which settled on each one of them. 4 And they were all filled (diffused throughout their souls) with the Holy Spirit and began to speak in other (different, foreign) languages (tongues), as the Spirit kept giving them clear and loud expression [in each tongue in appropriate words]." Acts 2:1-4 Amplified Version

This is one of the most powerful benefits we will experience as we pray in tongues; not just individually but as a corporate assembly. Acts 2 takes us on a journey that continues from Acts 1:13-14. This is where a corporate gathering occurred and 120 believers met in an upper room. They continued there with one accord in prayer and supplication until the manifestation of the Spirit of Promise, the Comforter whom Jesus prophesied, had come and made His grand appearance. Now verse 1 of chapter 2 brings us to a place called "The Fullness." Here on the day of Pentecost, according to the prophetic calendar of God, an eternal release came into the earth. The Spirit of God was being poured out so that all who would come to partake of God's redemptive power through Jesus could have the Holy Spirit to live inside them. Verses 2-3 gives us two important aspects that are worthy of observation. They are *"the sounds of a rushing mighty wind"* and *"the appearance of cloven tongues of fire."* The concept of hearing and speaking are very important in praying in tongues.

In my years of working with intercessors, the greatest challenge has been getting them to incline their ears to hear the sounds of heaven and then to speak what they have heard in the place of prayer. This inability, unfortunately, has caused the Church to lack as it relates to having power in fulfilling our commission. Praying in tongues causes a stirring in the heavens whereby God will begin to give us sounds that will ultimately give life to His desires in our land. This scene in the book of Acts had been prophesied by Joel hundreds of years before the fulfillment. I believe that prayer, especially praying in tongues, is vital if we are to experience the outpouring of the promises of God. There are certain things that are active in the realm of the Spirit that have yet to find access in the earth. Praying in tongues is the link to release heavens desires in earth through a covenant people. Isaiah 30:30 declares:

"And the Lord shall cause His glorious voice to be heard, and shall show the lightning down of His arm, with the indignation of his anger, and with the flame of a devouring fire, with scattering, and tempest, and hailstones."

This verse gives us keys as to why we must hear and release the voice of the Lord accurately. As we speak what we hear, the Lord can ultimately show his arm which represents salvation. His indignation will come as a devouring fire which represents the presence of God; for our God is a consuming fire. Finally, accurately speaking the voice of the Lord produces scattering, tempest and hailstones, all products of wind. The sounds of heaven will produce wind and fire as we pray from that place of hearing clearly; suddenly, Him who we seek will make His appearance as the God who answers by fire.

BENEFIT #3

PRAYING IN TONGUES STRENGTHENS OUR WEAKNESSES

"Likewise the Spirit also helpeth our infirmities: for we know not what we should pray for as we ought: but the Spirit Himself maketh intercession for us with groanings which cannot be uttered. 27 And he that searcheth the hearts knoweth what is the mind of the Spirit, because he maketh intercession for the Saints according to the will of God. 28 And we know that all things work together for good to them that love God, to them who are called according to his purpose. Romans 8:26-28

These verses carry a powerful truth that is progressive in its nature and worthy of being followed by all believers. The scripture gives us a key to become strengthened by the Spirit of God through allowing Him to have liberty by praying through us with groanings, deep sighs and inexpressible yearnings. As we yield our vocal cords to this operation, we will see strength come to the frailties within our lives and within the lives of those we are praying for. Jesus declared that "the Spirit of Truth (Holy Spirit) has been sent by the Father to lead us and guide us into all truth" and He also has a responsibility to show us things to come.

Mankind has always experienced weaknesses; especially in the areas of seeking guidance and knowing of future events. Because of such weaknesses, the devil has been able to prosper his kingdom in the earth. The enemy has been more than faithful to accommodate us by establishing psychic networks and a whole barrage of other demonically-inspired works to resolve the issues of humanity. Therefore, the Church must rise up and allow the Holy Spirit to do His job as we yield to Him by praying in tongues. When we yield to the Holy Spirit and give Him expression in praying through us; our weaknesses, impasses, deadlocks, fears, and drawbacks in completing divine assignments will be broken and a kingdom release of grace will be our portion.

Many have viewed praying in tongues as being only supernaturally inspired. Yes, this is partly true; but as with anything else that is required of us by God, we must have a work to accompany our faith. As in the natural, we have language that is considered our own and we do not need divine inspiration to speak it. Yet, many of us do need divine inspiration to refrain from speaking too much. However, this is not the case with praying by speaking in tongues. It is a language that is given to us by God. He should not have to always inspire us to communicate with Him. We as believers should take advantage of the opportunity we have to directly communicate with Him.

We also discover that the Spirit of God searches our

hearts and has knowledge of what is in the mind of the Spirit. His prayer through us is according to the will of God. Praying in tongues, according to this verse, is actually one of the purest forms of prayer because it is the will of God. I have heard many people say, "I don't know what the will of God is for my life" or you'll hear them ask, "Has the Lord showed you anything about what I am called to do?" The faithless list of responses as to why believers are unsure of their roles in life can go on for pages, but a simple act of obedience, allowing the Holy Ghost to use our voices and pray through us, is all that is needed. This goes against our intellect, which is usually the main stronghold that hinders us from flowing in the Holy Spirit.

The final truth regarding this benefit is found in verse 28, where a connection of all things that pertain to our life in God will start working in harmony for our good. This is because when we love God, we will obey Him. The Bible declares in II Peter 1:3, *"According as His divine power hath given unto us all things that pertain unto life and godliness, through the knowledge of him that hath called us to glory and virtue."* Therefore as we give ourselves to prayer, God is more than faithful to accommodate us by causing weaknesses in our lives to be exposed and compensating us with strength to overcome and live victoriously.

BENEFIT #4

PRAYING IN TONGUES BRINGS FORTH HIDDEN WISDOM

⁶Howbeit we speak wisdom among them that are perfect: yet not the wisdom of this world, nor of the princes of this world, that come to nought: ⁷But we speak the wisdom of God in a mystery, even the hidden wisdom, which God ordained before the world unto our glory: ⁸Which none of the princes of this world knew: for had they known it, they would not have crucified the Lord of glory. ⁹But as it is written, Eye hath not seen, nor ear heard, neither have entered into the heart of man, the things which God hath prepared for them that love him. ¹⁰But God hath revealed them unto us by his Spirit: for the Spirit searcheth all things, yea, the deep things of God. ¹¹For what man knoweth the things of a man, save the spirit of man which is in him? even so the things of God knoweth no man, but the Spirit of God. ¹²Now we have received, not the spirit of the world, but the spirit which is of God; that we might know the things that are freely given to us of God. ¹³Which things also we speak, not in the words which man's wisdom teacheth, but which the Holy Ghost teacheth; comparing spiritual things with spiritual.

I Corinthians 2:6-13

Let us examine various verses in I Corinthians 2 and explore the value associated with speaking and releasing God's wisdom. Verse six declares, *"howbeit we speak wisdom among them that are perfect: yet not the wisdom of this world, nor of the princes of this world, that come to nought."* In this passage, we find that as we speak God's wisdom it brings us into maturity in Him. The wisdom of God gained gives believers a favorable edge over our enemies. Through godly wisdom, the effectiveness of the world's system and carnal intelligence are neutralized. The powers of darkness and the prince of this world are judged impotent. II Timothy 2:7 says *"Consider what I say; and the Lord give thee understanding in all things."* Without considering what is being said by the wisdom of God, difficulty in understanding is inevitable. As it relates to prayer, we need the wisdom of God to be released through us so that our understanding can be fruitful in all things.

I Corinthians 2:7 states, *"but we speak the wisdom of God in a mystery, even the hidden wisdom which God ordained before the world unto our glory."* One of the ways we can speak God's wisdom in a mystery according to I Corinthians 14:2 is by praying in tongues. The full measure of God's wisdom is made available to be released to us as we pray in tongues. The Holy Spirit becomes involved in our requests being brought to the Father and His counsel being brought back to us. We serve as vehicles for the Spirit of God to have expression. This is a Kingdom mystery. This exchange of mutual dialogue is free from demonic interference. The forces of hell cannot eavesdrop on these divine conversations. This is truly a weapon that will strengthen the warfare of the saints. It is understandable why the enemy of our soul is attacking the use of our heavenly prayer language. If he can bring controversy and confusion in use of this gift, then he has won a great battle. God is removing the fears and stigmas of His gifts to His Body.

The Apostle Paul talks about "the things of God not being seen, heard, or entering into our *hearts*" in verse nine. The heart is the seat of all of our dreams, aspirations, fears, and thoughts. It is in the heart, where we ponder the questions of life. The Word of God also declares in Matthew 12:34b that ..."*Out of the abundance of the heart the mouth speaks.*" Our hearts have become the source of our words. This is the place where the New Covenant has been established with God. When God is truly within the believer's heart, we will see those things He has prepared for us manifest in our lives. The Holy Spirit begins to articulate the Heart of God to his people through this divine exchange of praying in tongues. He explores "deep things of God" and brings insight and wisdom into the hearts of the saints. He releases present truth and revelation needed for the moment. He knows what we have need of and is there to meet our needs.

There are great needs within our global communities and governments which will continue to go unmet until we begin to tap into the wisdom of God. We are living in a day when time is no longer on our side. The earth is full of wars and rumors of wars. Anxiety and depression are rampant. Divorce and chaos are in our homes; overwhelming many and threatening the sanctity of family unit. Yet, I believe our only source of hope is in the Wisdom of God. Therefore the Church must begin to gather corporately and continue to cry out for God's wisdom to flood the earth.

BENEFIT #5

PRAYING IN TONGUES BRINGS UNDERSTANDING TO MYSTERIES

"For he that speaketh in an unknown tongue speaketh not onto men, but unto God: for no man understandeth him: howbeit in the spirit he speaketh mysteries."

I Corinthians 14:2

Within these verses, we discover more truths regarding praying in tongues. The Apostle Paul identifies who is the creator and recipient of this type of dialogue. He begins to clarify the purpose and the expected outcome to be gained by praying in tongues. As one prays in tongues, he is conversing with God. In this spiritual conversation, there is an exchange of wisdom and secrets. The individual that prays in his spiritual prayer language is strengthened and encouraged in his inner man. One of the lies the devil tells is that we should not speak in tongues except there is an interpreter. This lie has caused many to lack in power, wisdom and revelation by the omission of this spiritual gift.

There was a move of God that took place in the early 1900's that was known as the Azusa Revival. The Spirit of God was poured out on the Church and believers from many ethnic groups. They were filled with the Holy Ghost and spoke in unknown tongues.

This move of God took place during a time of deep racial, economic and social division; yet God caused the Church to rise above those biases. This move of the Spirit began to stir His people to pray together in unknown tongues. As the people gathered together, praying in unknown tongues, God challenged the social ills of that day and brought unity among many people. Without the Holy Spirit having access and the liberty to challenge us in our personal lives and core values, as on Azusa Street in California, strife among the ethnic groups will continue to increase. We can gather much insight from this brief history lesson concerning the Church and the conditions of our land. In spite of all of our humanistic endeavors, our wisdom will come to naught without knowing how to connect with God in prayer.

Praying in tongues strengthens us in our spiritual walk. There are mysteries of the Kingdom, which God has commanded us to know. Matthew 13:11 declares, *He answered and said unto them, Because it is given unto you to know the mysteries of the kingdom of heaven, but to them it is not given.* The gift of praying in tongues is essential in discovering and fulfilling our assignments. As we exercise this gift, puzzling questions are answered and new revelations are also imparted to us by the Spirit of God.

BENEFIT #6

PRAYING IN TONGUES ACTIVATES
SPIRITUAL GIFTS

"Now brethren, if I come unto you speaking with tongues, what shall I profit you, except I shall speak to you either by revelation, or by knowledge, or by prophesying, or by doctrine?"   *I Corinthians 14:6*

This passage of scripture gives four specific areas of how we can benefit by praying in tongues. The first is gaining revelation. Believers need revelation to be released by the Spirit of God into our lives. This will enable us to move in greater realms of accuracy, as it relates to the call of God upon our lives. There are certain dimensions of authority and grace that the Church, as a whole, will never operate in apart from revelation. The word, "revelation" is derived from the word "reveal" which means *"to make known, to uncover or disclose something that is hidden."* Proverbs 25:2 declares that *"It's the glory of God to conceal (hide) a thing but it is the honor of kings to search out a matter."* The word, "matter" in the Hebrew language in this verse, literally means *"a word, thing, or cause as spoken of."* The Lord has made us kings and priests. We have a responsibility to search out and disclose His glory by obtaining revelation of the things that He is declaring in the earth for the Church.

The Apostle Paul in Ephesians 1:17-18 prayed for the church of Ephesus *"to be given the spirit of wisdom and revelation in the knowledge of Jesus and for the eyes of their understanding to be enlightened and that they would know the hope of His calling and the riches of His glory in the saints."* There are many things concerning the Kingdom of God we will never understand apart from having His revelation upon our lives. Praying in tongues is one way of unlocking the mysteries of the Kingdom. Revelation also helps to sustain, enhance and advance our lives. Revelation opens our understanding to the deep things of the Spirit. There is also a release of power that helps to establish the Church by the preaching of the gospel of Jesus Christ according to the revelation of mysteries. *"Now to him that is of power to stablish you according to my gospel, and the preaching of Jesus Christ, according to the revelation of the mystery, which was kept secret since the world began,"* Romans 16:25

Knowledge is another area that believers can profit from by praying in tongues. The word, "knowledge" is defined as *"an awareness or familiarity of or with a person or thing, understanding of a subject, range of information."* There is a level of understanding concerning the things of the Spirit that God desires His children to walk in. There are certain spiritual realms that the Church needs to embrace in levels of knowledge that can only be obtained by the Spirit of God. As humans, we are full of inadequacies in our own strength; yet as we yield to the direction of the Holy Ghost, supernatural insight is obtained. Proverbs 11:9 declares *"A hypocrite with his mouth destroyeth his neighbor, but through knowledge shall the just be delivered."* Deliverance ministry is a vital part of the Church today. Many individuals come to our churches on a regular basis and are bound by demonic spirits in various areas of their lives. It takes knowledge to set captives free and many believers continue to stay bound and defeated because of this void. One of the gifts of the Spirit is the Word of Knowledge. We can see the importance of praying in tongues and being able to activate spiritual gifts to set the captives free.

Proverbs 24:4-5 declares *"And by knowledge shall the chambers be filled with all precious and pleasant riches. A wise man is strong; yea, a man of knowledge increases strength."* By spending time praying in tongues, believers can acquire knowledge and receive power to fill areas in our lives that are lacking; thereby causing precious and pleasant riches to be built within us. It is one thing to have a wealth of resources; but it is another thing to have our lives filled with the precious and pleasant things of God.

Prophesying is another area where God desires for the Church to excel. The word, "prophesy" means *to declare, tell forth, or reveal the Word of the Lord."* It can also be defined as *"the act of predicting the future as inspired by the anointing of the Lord."* All believers should prophesy. There are four realms whereby we can prophesy. They are:

- *The prophecy of the scriptures. (II Peter 1: 20-21)*
- *The gift of prophecy. (I Corinthians 12:10)*
- *The spirit of prophecy. (Revelations 19:10)*
- *The office of prophet. (I Corinthians 12:28)*

All believers should flow in prophetic ministry according to I Corinthians 14:3. I Corinthians 14:25 reveals how prophecy can unveil the secrets of a person's heart. *"And thus are the secrets of his heart made manifest; and so falling down on his face he will worship God, and report that God is in you of a truth."* I believe that as we pray in tongues, the Spirit of God will show us the matters or concerns of a person's heart; and in return we can prophesy. Through praying in tongues, believers can bring edification for those who need to be built up, exhortation for those who need to be encouraged, and comfort for those who need joy and life by the word of God. This is an area where God really wants His Church to grow and mature. The prophetic, as stated, is given to bring a greater measure of accuracy and excellence to the Body of Christ through the Voice of the Lord. This increase is contingent on the willingness of the saints to speak the mysteries of the kingdom by praying in tongues.

Sound doctrine is the fourth area the Church can

benefit from by praying in tongues. It is imperative for the Church to grow in the grace of God and become more assertive in utilizing the things of the Spirit. There are many individuals who desire to teach and preach the Word of God who have no prayer life. One of the ways to be strengthened in the area of our doctrine is to pray in tongues. Praying in tongues carries a divine strength that will cause our doctrine to take on levels of soundness necessary to resist the pull of false teaching and deception that are wide spread in the earth today. The word, "doctrine", is defined as *"teachings, what's taught, body of instructions."* The scripture challenges us in II Timothy 2:15, *"Study that we might show ourselves approved unto God as workman that needeth not be ashamed, rightly dividing the word of truth."* Because we are admonished to study for the purpose of accuracy, we can build on the fact that prayer will help fulfill this mandate. Therefore, we can move from revelation to knowledge, from knowledge to prophesying, from prophesying to sound doctrine as a result of praying in tongues.

BENEFIT #7

PRAYING IN TONGUES RELEASES HOLINESS

"Beloved, when I gave all diligence to write unto you of the common salvation, it was needful for me to write unto you, and exhort you that ye should earnestly contend for the faith which was once delivered unto the saints. For there are certain men crept in unawares, who were before of old ordained to this condemnation, ungodly men, turning the grace of our God into lasciviousness, and denying the only Lord God, and our Lord Jesus Christ."

Jude 1:3-4

"But ye, beloved, building up yourselves on your most holy faith, praying in the Holy Ghost, keep yourselves in the love of God, looking for the mercy of our Lord Jesus Christ unto eternal life."

Jude 1: 20-21

There is a real battle taking place concerning the work of salvation that the Lord Jesus accomplished in the earth. God requires that the saints live holy and pure lives. Yet, we find ourselves being dragged into courts where justice systems are perverted and used to promote moral discrepancies. There are believers, worshipping in churches today, that are receiving doctrines and teaching from preachers, which are actually promoted by devils. This demonic invasion is definitely on the rise in America. Jude foresaw a company of ungodly men releasing unbridled lust through their teachings within the Church. By the time we arrive to verse 20, all manner of uncleanness is activated. The key to the Church, escaping this influx of perversion, is to build ourselves up to a level of faith; which is called *"most holy faith."* This can be done by praying in the Holy Ghost. There is a level of utterance that the Church will ascend to, as we intercede. I believe that most, if not all, battles being fought today concerning purity have to do with the lack of power the church truly walks in. Praying in tongues releases a grace that will cause us to rise above and beyond the uncleanness that is asserting itself in the earth. The Lord Himself declared in Matthew 16:18 *"And I say unto thee, That thou art Peter, and upon this rock I will build my **CHURCH**; and the gates of hell shall not prevail against it."* The fulfillment of this word is going to require a level of faith our generation has yet to see. I believe praying in the Holy Ghost is one of the catalyst needed to cause this word to manifest in the earth.

BENEFIT #8

THE DIMENSIONS OF INTERCESSION: ASKING, SEEKING & KNOCKING

"Ask, and it shall be given you; seek, and ye shall find; knock, and it shall be opened unto you: For every one that asketh receiveth; and he that seeketh findeth; and to him that knocketh it shall be opened." Matthew 7:7-8

We have revealed several benefits given by God as we pray in tongues. This final benefit I want to address helps to strengthen the reality of all the others. Jesus makes it clear, if we ask, it shall be given. The right requests will warrant the right response. The scriptures declare *"Ye ask, and receive not, because ye ask amiss, that ye may consume it upon your lusts"* James 4:3. When we make righteous requests, we will be able to seek God with purity, and the doors we knock on will open for us.

In Matthew 7:7-8, Jesus unveils a pattern for intercession. Believers need this revelation to implement and activate truths from the word of God for divine results. The word "implement" means *"to carry out, execute, perform, bring to pass, to put into effect."* The word "activate" means *"to turn on, initiate, stir up, fire up, to set in motion."* Our intercession must become an avenue to bless the earth and convey the answers to problems that are plaguing our nations.

There are three realms of prayer in which the saints can access to release the power of God. The first realm or level of intercession identified by Jesus is to *"ask."* The definition of the word, "ask" is *"to inquire of, to request information about, to demand, to expect, or to invite."* This type of intercession creates an atmosphere for God the Father to fulfill requests and release resources. I like to connect the act of asking to the offering of prayers of supplication. Zechariah 12:10 declares that God *"would pour upon the house of David and upon the inhabitants of Jerusalem the spirit of grace and of supplications."* I am convinced that in the place of prayer we need the spirit of grace (God's favor) to make the right supplication (requests).

If the saints do not rise up and ask God for His will to be enforced in the territories we inhabit, then the days ahead will be days of fear and dread. Psalm 115:16 declares *"the heaven, even the heavens, are the Lord's: but the earth hath he given to the children of men."* As we ask for the power of God to be released, this is exactly what we will receive. We must come to the place of receiving revelation, which will enlighten the eyes of our understanding. Revelation when released whether by preaching, teaching or in the place of prayer activates the spirit of faith and power. So, rise up Saints of the Most High and know that as we ask of Him, it is His good pleasure to give us the Kingdom!

The second realm or level mentioned by Jesus is to

"seek." The word, "seek" means *"to try to find, to discover, to try to obtain."* This realm of prayer is equated to Prophetic Intercession. When the Church unleashes this kind of prayer, the Father begins to reveal what is on His mind and proclaims His counsel. Prophetic intercession does not come with set guidelines or established perimeters. Unlike informed intercession which is prayer released based on what we know or have learned, prophetic intercession is established on what is on the mind of God revealed by the Holy Spirit. Praying in tongues, by unction, by impression, by open vision and by revelation are all manifestations of prophetic intercession.

Jesus engaged this dimension of intercession in the garden of Gethsemane when He began to utter Matthew 26:39: *"And he went a little farther, and fell on his face, and prayed, saying, O my Father, if it be possible, let this cup pass from me: nevertheless not as I will, but as thou wilt."* He proclaimed "Nevertheless, not as I will but Thy will be done." Prophetically, His pursuit in prayer was for God's counsel or mind to come forth. This request, while in a seek mode, caused divine alignment to infiltrate Gethsemane. The Greek definition for Gethsemane is "oil press." It was through seeking, while in the oil press of Gethsemane, God's ordained will for Jesus' life was settled.

The third realm or level mentioned by Jesus is to

"**knock**." The word, "knock" means *"to strike with a sharp or hard blow, to collide or cause to collide with, to be rough and brutal with, and to disassemble into parts."* This realm is equated to warfare prayer which is one of my personal favorites. Growing up on the rugged streets of the Westside of Chicago, "knocking" was a common thing. The Body of Christ has been commissioned to launch warfare against the kingdoms of darkness. When we look at the word "warfare" from II Corinthians 10:4: *"For the weapons of our warfare are not carnal, but mighty through God to the pulling down of strongholds."* Its root is derived from a Greek word called **"strateia"** (Strong's Concordance #4752 – 4754). This language illustrates the apostolic career - one of hardship and danger. Apostolic believers live to contend with the powers of darkness in warfare prayer. In the realm of knocking (warfare), there is a grace to bring the saints together in corporate gatherings for the purpose of disassembling the powers of darkness. There are doors to nations, regions and people groups which will not open except for the prayers of those who will contend in prayer. Paul encouraged the church of Colossae to

"Continue in prayer, and watch in the same with thanksgiving; withal praying also for us, that God would open unto us a door of utterance, to speak the mystery of Christ, for which I am also in bonds: That I may make it manifest, as I ought to speak." Colossians 4:2-4.

The Apostle Paul understood that if he was to declare the mysteries in his region, a door in the Spirit must be opened. The words apostles release in the earth will always bring direction, clarity, encouragement, wisdom, and upgrade in the lives of believers. If the earth is to become a recipient of these blessings, doors of utterance can only be opened through warfare prayer. We must rise to the occasion for our generation and give life to the things that God has ordained by asking, seeking, and knocking in the place of prayer.

CONCLUSION

Being kept and guarded by the love of God are spontaneous rewards for believers through the gift of salvation. We will have an accurate view of the Lord's mercy and the eternal benefits of God will be ours. Saints of God, the gift of praying in tongues served as the vehicle God used to bring His Church into the earth at Pentecost. Praying in tongues is still the means that the Lord is using to help His Church prevail in the earth. Prayer is a vital part in helping to assure the return of the Lord. It is my prayer to see Intercession through the speaking in tongues released around the earth; while ascending and filling the heavenly skies above. It is in this flow of worship and intercession that the people of God will hasten the glorious coming of our King! *If you desire to know more and experience this wonderful gift from our Heavenly Father, please pray this simple prayer:*

Father in the name of Jesus,

I desire to receive a fresh baptism of the Holy Ghost and fire. I ask you to fill me with the gift of a prayer language from the Spirit of God. I renounce all barriers that restrict and hinder me from expressing the mysteries of the Spirit of God. I decree my tongue has become that of a pen of a ready writer. I proclaim over my life that out of my belly rivers of living water are flowing and that these waters have a spring that release gladness in the earth. Lord, I thank you for the new levels and benefits that have been given to me. I decree the release of revelation, knowledge, prophesy, and doctrine over my life. I now claim a release of the Kingdom of God into my prophetic journey that impacts my destiny and the destiny of nations! In Jesus' name, Amen.

More Great Resources from
Rivers of Living Water

Books
- Apostolic Pioneering
- Benefits of Praying in Tongues
- Exposing the Spirit of Anger
- Fundamentals of Deliverance 101
- Ministering Spirits: "Engaging the Angelic Realm"
- Pray Without Ceasing
- Pray Without Ceasing Volume II
- Restoring Prophetic Watchmen

CD's
- Prayers For The Nations CD
- Prayers Against Python &.Witchcraft
- Prayers Of Healing & Restoration CD
- Thy Kingdom Come CD
- Latter Rain CD
- Overcoming Spirits of Terrorism CD
- Songs of Intercession

**Visit Our On-line Ministry Bookstore at
www.rolwchicago.com
Or contact us at for additional information**
Phone 773.826.1442
Email: rolw@sbcglobal.net

Contact Information

Rivers of Living Water
Ministries International Chicago
2948 W Madison Ave
Chicago, IL 60612

Mailing Address
P.O. Box 528142
Chicago, IL 60652

Phone 773.826.1442
Fax 773.498.4343
Email: rolw@sbcglobal.net

For more of Apostle Garner's inspiring messages, visit our website at www.rolwchicago.com